My Neighborhood

by Barbara L. Luciano

Editorial Offices: Glenview, Illinois • Parsippany, New Jersey • New York, New York
Sales Offices: Needham, Massachusetts • Duluth, Georgia • Glenview, Illinois
Coppell, Texas • Sacramento, California • Mesa, Arizona

We live in a community.

Some communities are in the city.
They are large.

A suburb has many homes and families.

Some communities are in the country.
They may be small.

Many communities have streets, houses, stores, and signs.

What is your community like?

Glossary

community where people live

country community where few
people live

sign something that gives people
information

store place to buy things

suburb community with homes
and stores